Special Days

May Day

Clare Chandler

WAYLAND

►Special Days◄

Bonfire Night
May Day
Mother's Day
Poppy Day

Editor: Carron Brown
Series design: Kate Buxton
Book designer: Joyce Chester
Illustrator: David Antram
Consultant: Norah Granger

First published in 1998 by Wayland Publishers Limited,
61 Western Road, Hove, East Sussex, BN3 1JD

Find Wayland on the Internet at http://www.wayland.co.uk

British Library Cataloguing in Publication Data
Chandler, Clare
May Day. – (Special Days)
1. May Day – Juvenile literature
2. May Day – History – Juvenile literature
I. Title II. Antram, David
394.2'697

ISBN 0 7502 2082 1

Typeset in England by Joyce Chester
Printed and bound by G. Canale and C.S.p.A in Turin, Italy

Picture Acknowledgements
The publishers would like to thank the following for allowing us to reproduce their pictures:
Bridgeman Art Library, London/Christopher Wood Gallery, London 20, /Museum of the City of New York 14;
Britstock – IFA/Stephen Gabriel 22; E. T. Archive/British Museum 8; Robert Harding/Jeremy Bright 4, /Adam Woolfitt 9;
Hulton Getty 12, 23; Image Bank 26; Oxfordshire County Libraries 21; The Scotsman Publications Ltd 11;
Tony Stone/Christopher Ameson 5, /Richard Passmore 15; Trip/J. Ringland *title page*, 19, /N. and J. Wiseman 27.

Contents

May Day

May Day is the first day of the month of May. For many people it is a special day, and in some countries it is a holiday for everyone.

After the long, cold winter and the warm spring, summer is about to arrive.

▼ Bluebells are in flower at the beginning of May.

▲ Most farm animals have their babies in spring or early summer.

Plants are growing and flowering, and baby animals are being born.

May Day is a time to celebrate new life and growth.

How May Day began

There have always been celebrations at this time of the year to welcome the new life and encourage everything to grow.

The Ancient Romans believed in a goddess of the spring called Flora.

▼ The Romans held a festival for the coming of Spring. They believed that the goddess Flora breathed flowers over the countryside.

When Flora breathed, flowers came out of her mouth and spread across the countryside. The Roman people held a wild and merry festival for her every year at the beginning of May.

The festival of Beltane

The ancient people of Britain used to celebrate on the night before May Day. The festival was called Beltane.

▼ A Druid priest.

Their priests, who were called Druids, built large bonfires high up on hills.

At the end of the festival, people herded their cattle between the fires. They believed that the cattle would then be free from disease for the rest of the year.

▲ This ancient circle of stones is called Stonehenge. People think it was once a Druids' temple.

Beltane was first celebrated in Scotland. Later it became popular in Wales and Ireland too.

Everyone gathered around a bonfire and ate a special meal. Then they sang songs and danced together until late in the night. In central Scotland, Beltane is still an important festival.

▼ On the evening of the last day in April, many people gather on Carlton Hill in Edinburgh to celebrate Beltane.

▲ The May Queen and her handmaidens at the Beltane celebrations in Edinburgh.

Scaring witches

People used to think that witches flew around the sky on the night before May Day doing evil things. They believed that fire would frighten the witches away.

◀ Long ago, people believed that witches flew through the night sky.

As well as building bonfires, men and women sometimes ran around the fields with blazing torches.

▼ On the Isle of Man, people used to set light to gorse bushes, hoping to scare off any witches.

Party time

May Day was a holiday for everyone.
It used to be celebrated with parties in
the streets, races, archery contests and
morris dancing.

▼ Everyone used to join in the
May Day festivities.

You will still see morris dancing in many parts of Britain. The dancers usually wear white and black costumes with bells tied to their legs. They wave handkerchiefs or knock sticks together, and the bells jingle as they stamp and kick their legs.

▲ Morris dancing is a very old tradition.

The maypole

In the past, a maypole stood at the centre of every town and village on May Day. It was a tall, thin tree with its branches cut off. The trunk was painted and decorated with flowers, sweet-smelling herbs and colourful ribbons. It looked beautiful.

▼ The girls who danced around the maypole wore white dresses and had flowers in their hair.

Everyone danced around the maypole, plaiting the ribbons around the pole as they danced.

17

The May tree

Early on May Day morning everyone went out and collected branches from the May tree. This tree, which is also called hawthorn, has masses of strong-smelling white or pink flowers during May.

▼ Collecting branches from the May tree.

18

People used to think this tree had magical powers. They put its branches outside their barns to make their cows produce more milk.

▲ On May Day some people dress like this. They are called Jack-in-the-Greens.

May garlands

Children used to make garlands from
May trees with their milky-white flowers.
Sometimes, they went from house to house
with their garlands, singing songs and
collecting money.

▼ This photograph was taken
on May Day nearly a hundred
years ago.

◄ Children with their May Day garlands.

Another custom was to fix plants to people's doors. Plants were chosen whose names rhymed with the character of the person. Holly was for someone jolly, briar for a liar and plum for anyone who was glum.

King and Queen of the May

One of the main events of the day used to be the crowning of the May Queen. A girl was chosen to be queen. She was crowned with wild flowers and led the parade through the streets.

Some places also had a May King. He was usually the boy who won the race to the May tree.

◀ A May Queen crowned with roses.

▲ A May Queen in 1923, wearing a crown
decorated with spring flowers.

Obby Oss

Some towns and villages have special ways of celebrating May Day. At Padstow in Cornwall, May Day is still a lively festival. Everyone turns out to see a strange hobby-horse that dances through the streets to the music of drums and accordions.

The 'Obby Oss', as they call it, is a man covered in black material with a little horse's head in front. But on his face is a furry mask with a fierce snapping beak and a large red tongue.

▼ The Obby Oss winds its way up a crowded street in Padstow, Cornwall.

Labour Day

In 1889, May Day was chosen as International Labour Day. It was a special day for workers everywhere. In China, it is still an important holiday.

◀ In China, people celebrate May Day with beautiful firework displays like this one.

In Britain, May Day is celebrated on the first Monday of the month of May. It is a bank holiday, when most people do not go to work and many of the shops are closed.

▲ A May Day parade in Moscow, Russia.

Welcome the summer

May Day is a good time to welcome the summer. Look out for May blossoms in parks and hedgerows. There may be a maypole or morris dancers in a town or village near you. You might even see a May Queen being crowned.

▼ A May Day street party in England.

28

Every year, as the weather becomes warmer, there is new life everywhere. May Day is a time to celebrate!

Glossary

Accordion   A musical instrument with a keyboard that is carried by a musician.

Archery   The sport of shooting with a bow and arrows.

Garland   Flowers or leaves bound together in a circle.

Gorse   A large prickly plant with bright yellow flowers.

Herbs   Plants that are used in cookery and medicine, such as parsley, rosemary and thyme.

Hobby-horse   A toy horse. It is usually a stick with a horse's head on the top.

Puritan   A person who lived in the seventeenth century. He or she had very strict ideas about how people should behave.

Timeline

The Romans (753 BC–AD 395)	Romans celebrate the festival of Flora at the beginning of May.
From 600 BC	Ancient Britons celebrate Beltane on May Day eve.
The Middle Ages (1066–1500)	May Day is a popular festival in Britain.
1644	Maypoles are banned by the Puritans.
1660	Charles II becomes king and the maypoles are put back. A maypole which is 40 metres high is put up in London.
1889	May Day becomes International Labour Day.
1978	The first year that Britain has a bank holiday to celebrate Labour Day on the first Monday of May.

Further information

For younger readers
Every Year: A Sense of History by Sallie Purkis (Longman, 1995)
Get Set Go: Spring Festivals by Helen Bliss (Watts, 1995)

For older readers
Summer Festivals by Mike Rosen (Wayland, 1990)
Why Do We Celebrate That? by Jane Wilcox (Franklin Watts, 1996)

Places to visit
These are some of the towns and villages which have special May Day celebrations: Padstow in Cornwall; Minehead in Somerset; Oxford; Durham; Edinburgh (May Day eve). The festivals are either on the first day of May or on the first Monday of the month.

Index